© **THE WAY TO GO IS FORWARD**
BY SANDEEP RAVIDUTT SHARMA

Table of Contents

Introduction IV

The Way To Go Is Forward...1

© **THE WAY TO GO IS FORWARD**
BY SANDEEP RAVIDUTT SHARMA

Introduction

This book presents you with a list of **100 motivational quotes** written with the blessings and grace of Goddess Bhairavi. I'm sure if you keep reading, referring, sharing these thoughts and quotes, you will draw motivation and develop a good understanding of various perspectives and facts of life. Life is a journey, and the only way to go is forward. Keep going with a smile on your face and kindness in your heart. Each step forward brings you closer to your destination. The world awaits you with a bouquet of joy and happiness to cheer you at your destination. Look beyond your destination as you march again for the next one.

"As you follow in the footsteps of the learned, you will find that it is pointing forward. Look back only when someone calls you for help or the past motivates you to move forward."

I sincerely hope, you will find this book amazing, interesting, rejuvenating, unique and constant source of motivation.

Thank You and Happy Reading.

© THE WAY TO GO IS FORWARD
BY SANDEEP RAVIDUTT SHARMA

© Copyright 2018 Sandeep Ravidutt Sharma - All rights reserved.

In no way is it legal to reproduce, duplicate, or transmit any part of this document in either electronic means or in printed format. Recording of this publication is strictly prohibited and any storage of this document is not allowed unless with written permission from the publisher. All rights reserved.

The information provided herein is stated to be truthful and consistent, in that any liability, in terms of inattention or otherwise, by any usage or abuse of any policies, processes, or directions contained within is the solitary and utter responsibility of the recipient reader. Under no circumstances will any legal responsibility or blame be held against the author / publisher for any reparation, damages, or monetary loss due to the information herein, either directly or indirectly. The author own all copyrights.

Legal Notice:
This book is copyright protected. This is only for personal use. You cannot amend, distribute, sell, use, quote or paraphrase any part or the content within this book without the consent of the author or copyright owner. Legal action will be pursued if this is breached.

Disclaimer Notice:
Please note the information contained within this book is for motivational, educational and knowledge sharing purpose only. Every attempt has been made to provide the reader accurate, up to date and reliable complete information. No warranties of any kind are expressed or implied. Readers acknowledge that the author is not engaging in the rendering of legal, financial, medical or professional advice. By reading this document, the reader agrees that under no circumstances the author / publisher is responsible for any losses, direct or indirect, which are incurred as a result of the use of information contained within this document, including, but not limited to, —errors, omissions, or inaccuracies.

If you have further questions, contact on
Tel: +919969256731
Email: sandeepraviduttsharma@gmail.com

© THE WAY TO GO IS FORWARD
BY SANDEEP RAVIDUTT SHARMA

Dedication

This book is dedicated to **Goddess Bhairavi**. In the Hindu religion, the Goddess Bhairavi represents divine anger and wrath which is directed towards impurities within us as well as to the negative forces that obstructs our spiritual growth. Bhairavi Mata is also called as **Shubhamkari** and does good things. She is often depicted in images as holding a book, rosary and making abhaya and varada mudra with her hands. She is fiercely protective, lending us wisdom and power, steadiness and clarity. She personifies light and fire, supporting us to reveal what we keep hidden and inviting us to explore our hidden mind and any secret darkness.

I hereby recite the following Bhairavi mool mantra...
"Om Hreem Bhairavi Kalaum Hreem Svaha"
And pray to **Goddess Bhairavi** for lending wisdom and power, steadiness and clarity in the life of my readers and the world. May Goddess Bhairavi protect us from negative forces along with removing impurities of our mind.

**THE WAY TO GO
IS FORWARD**

© **THE WAY TO GO IS FORWARD**
BY SANDEEP RAVIDUTT SHARMA

Time makes you invisible to some in the period of distress.

© THE WAY TO GO IS FORWARD
BY SANDEEP RAVIDUTT SHARMA

At times you can see the bridge that can take you to your destination. But the irony is you don't know how to reach the bridge. Keep Going... God makes the way.

If you believe in the existence of God and surrender all your karma to the almighty, then you don't have to even knock the door; the door of happiness, peace, calm and prosperity will always be open for you.

© THE WAY TO GO IS FORWARD
BY SANDEEP RAVIDUTT SHARMA

You need to overcome the fear of drowning in case swimming is your mission.

Friends are the ones who will push you into the swimming pool not just for fun but for making you to learn how to swim. Also, they will be the first to jump into the pool if they see you drowning.

© **THE WAY TO GO IS FORWARD**
BY SANDEEP RAVIDUTT SHARMA

Life doesn't allow any option sometimes. Be ready to go with the flow.

© **THE WAY TO GO IS FORWARD**
BY SANDEEP RAVIDUTT SHARMA

Some are enjoying life in the Sea while others in the Sky. Be ready to live joyfully on the ground.

© **THE WAY TO GO IS FORWARD**
BY SANDEEP RAVIDUTT SHARMA

Time changes the face of the man every second. Now it all depends on whether you care for your face or your soul.

© **THE WAY TO GO IS FORWARD**
BY SANDEEP RAVIDUTT SHARMA

Cheer up for today instead of crying for the past.

© **THE WAY TO GO IS FORWARD**
BY SANDEEP RAVIDUTT SHARMA

You can take on the world with your self-belief. Have deep trust in your own abilities and you can move mountains soon.

Overacting in life cannot last for long. Be real and you don't have to explain anything.

© THE WAY TO GO IS FORWARD
BY SANDEEP RAVIDUTT SHARMA

Even when the revered teachers are no more, the knowledge has stood the test of time and illuminate our path today and would continue in future.

© **THE WAY TO GO IS FORWARD**
BY SANDEEP RAVIDUTT SHARMA

If you believe in the spirit of humanity and have put in sincere efforts and kindness, someday you can create heaven on earth.

Be passionate about whatever you do. Results will be automatic.

© **THE WAY TO GO IS FORWARD**
BY SANDEEP RAVIDUTT SHARMA

Don't attempt to break the glass of sorrow with a stone of hatred. Instead, stir it with a spoon of Love. Sorrow will be no more.

The temptation to rise in life can put you in a fix while making choices. Forego the temptation and choose the right things even when it slows down your rise in life.

Hats off to the one who lives for bringing the smile on the face of the other.

Thoughts travel faster than light. In a split of a second, it reaches the next soul if you fail to retain it.

Those who are in the fray for gold have no other option except to showcase their brilliance outsmarting every other player.

Time discovers something new everytime. Time also covers everything under the carpet of history and reveals only to those who are interested in the past.

If you can't match pace with the current times, it's better to pave the way for the ones who can match it.

© **THE WAY TO GO IS FORWARD**
BY SANDEEP RAVIDUTT SHARMA

You can lie the whole world but can't lie your own self.

© **THE WAY TO GO IS FORWARD**
BY SANDEEP RAVIDUTT SHARMA

God takes a look at you. Be ready with your folded hands to pray and a beautiful smile to welcome the Lord.

Take a vow to face instead of bowing before the challenges. You become strong when you face challenges and not when you accept defeat without attempting to win.

The world ignored you but cannot hold it for long if you have the power to convince them about adopting your innovations.

Expectations like success while SUCCESS likes efforts.

© THE WAY TO GO IS FORWARD
BY SANDEEP RAVIDUTT SHARMA

Attract the best in life not through indulgence in luxurious pursuit but through things that can enrich your life and make it complete. Give your best contribution to humanity and reap the harvest of satisfaction, peace, rich life and blessings from the creator.

At times you can't see your own reflection forgot about claiming to know others.

God appears in various forms every moment. Only those who believe and are eager to meet can feel his presence in their lives.

Time makes you understand or let you just stand.

Shoot problems of the world by becoming a peacemaker rather than adding petrol in the burning fire.

© **THE WAY TO GO IS FORWARD**
BY SANDEEP RAVIDUTT SHARMA

Simple solutions for complex problems are not a joke but a possibility.

© **THE WAY TO GO IS FORWARD**
BY SANDEEP RAVIDUTT SHARMA

Change starts with you but never waits for you.

© **THE WAY TO GO IS FORWARD**
BY SANDEEP RAVIDUTT SHARMA

Hiding your smile creates a frowning effect on the other. While a wonderful smile is a return gift for the other.

Brilliance creates an impact. Give your best today and your brilliance can make you a winner and a role model for the world.

One can use light to illuminate the world or blind the other. The beautiful mind will choose to illuminate.

Sometimes it's good for you not to know about your destination. Knowing in advance about the pain and sufferings ahead can break you from within. By trusting the Lord and your inner strengths, you can face tomorrow full on.

© **THE WAY TO GO IS FORWARD**
BY SANDEEP RAVIDUTT SHARMA

At times you have to fight wars to establish peace. Gear up to win and save the world from cruel and tyrant rulers.

Time passes away so fast that someday you may not remember your own self.

The golden glow is forever for those who walk the path of positivity. Get inspiration from the sun, it not only glows but illuminates the world. The shine is shared with all those who are ready to receive.

Promise if you can deliver.

THE WAY TO GO IS FORWARD
BY SANDEEP RAVIDUTT SHARMA

You can draw inspiration not only from winners but losers as well and avoid mistakes which they have committed.

© **THE WAY TO GO IS FORWARD**
BY SANDEEP RAVIDUTT SHARMA

Dig treasure of Gold not outside but within your own self. Your rich thoughts and good deeds are more valuable than Gold.

Passion backs your knowledge and helps you to scale faster in life.

Holding grudge against others is the sure shot way of cultivating unhappiness. Forgive, and you become richer and happier every minute.

© **THE WAY TO GO IS FORWARD**
BY SANDEEP RAVIDUTT SHARMA

Peace comes from the calmness of mind.

Change is inevitable. Don't run away from change rather prepare yourself to keep pace with the change.

© **THE WAY TO GO IS FORWARD**
BY SANDEEP RAVIDUTT SHARMA

Do you have any regrets whatsoever? If yes! Express it with an open heart to the right person and release the load on your mind forever. It's better to get than regret.

Display courage at the right time. It not only wipes out the problem but motivates others as well.

© **THE WAY TO GO IS FORWARD**
BY SANDEEP RAVIDUTT SHARMA

Step out of your comfort zone to experience the world and beyond.

Believe in whatever you do, and success is ensured. To have a firm belief in your capability, all you need to have is pure thought and your masters' blessings in the form of knowledge and determination.

© THE WAY TO GO IS FORWARD
BY SANDEEP RAVIDUTT SHARMA

Innumerable thoughts keep visiting you every moment... But do you remember them all? According to me, it's a big No... you retain some and out of this implement few of them. Over a period of time, you tend to forget even the retained ones. The best way is to write it down or share it with others. This way good thoughts shared by you can benefit and inspire others.

© **THE WAY TO GO IS FORWARD**
BY SANDEEP RAVIDUTT SHARMA

Your mind decides whether you will win or lose...

It's your actions that has the power to shape your destiny.

Golden leaf is an illusion but many times we may like to live with it.

Act now if you are looking for the outcome.

© **THE WAY TO GO IS FORWARD**
BY SANDEEP RAVIDUTT SHARMA

Those who pay too much of importance to the future lose their today.

Nothing is lost if you managed to keep human values intact.

Your thoughts may create weapons of mass destruction. Your thoughts can also create heaven on earth. The choice is all yours.

Respect your parents and not their wealth.

You may know everything but not the critical ones due to which success stays away from you. After every failure understands and remembers the cause of it. And remember not to repeat the same mistake again.

God appears to be good or not in favour depending on your state of mind. To me, the creator is always in your favour and compassionate. If you believe this then you don't need anyone else to support you. Also, in that case, no power in this world can harm you.

© **THE WAY TO GO IS FORWARD**
BY SANDEEP RAVIDUTT SHARMA

You get what you ask for.

Run for your life in distress but walk gently for others, understanding their issue and taking a wise decision to save them.

Engage your mind in creating and not criticising.

You mind captures fascinating images of the beautiful life. Train your mind to retain good thoughts and ignore the ugly ones.

© **THE WAY TO GO IS FORWARD**
BY SANDEEP RAVIDUTT SHARMA

The power to turn the tables resides in your mind.

© **THE WAY TO GO IS FORWARD**
BY SANDEEP RAVIDUTT SHARMA

Gloomy thoughts may appear as if they are here to stay. Don't reserve a permanent place for them in your mind. Drive them out as soon as possible.

Contradictions are proof enough that we are humans. Accept your imperfections with a vow to achieve perfection someday.

© **THE WAY TO GO IS FORWARD**
BY SANDEEP RAVIDUTT SHARMA

Chase success in the right lane.

© **THE WAY TO GO IS FORWARD**
BY SANDEEP RAVIDUTT SHARMA

Hoist the flag of hope high enough for the losers to see and gear up to try again.

© **THE WAY TO GO IS FORWARD**
BY SANDEEP RAVIDUTT SHARMA

Yesterday's celebration cannot be reused again. Achieve and celebrate again.

© THE WAY TO GO IS FORWARD
BY SANDEEP RAVIDUTT SHARMA

When you feel no one is with you, remember the divine elements like the Sun, Moon, Star, and Mother Nature always accompany you whether you are in pain or enjoying your life.

As one grows old, anger gets replaced with patience because one has already experienced the after-effects of anger.

No wealth in the world is good enough to buy you calm and inner peace. It can just come when you attentively listen to the ringing bells and follow the sound till it disappears.

Be grateful to the people who could firmly hold your ladder of success.

© **THE WAY TO GO IS FORWARD**
BY SANDEEP RAVIDUTT SHARMA

The distraction of any kind can break your focus only when you have allowed it to.

© THE WAY TO GO IS FORWARD
BY SANDEEP RAVIDUTT SHARMA

Each day presents shock n surprises Every day cannot be the same. Sometimes you are driving in top gear on the highway and at other times you can't even pedal a bicycle. Accept your condition with a smile on your face. Do not get involved in the blame game. Time will change, and you are sure to win again.

Attract whatever you wish; wish whatever you like; like whatever your heart says and you can never go wrong.

© **THE WAY TO GO IS FORWARD**
BY SANDEEP RAVIDUTT SHARMA

You can't reach your destination if you have decided to run in the opposite direction. Align your actions with your aim.

Dreams define your path in the real world.

Bright ideas may lose its sheen if not executed in time or poorly executed.

© **THE WAY TO GO IS FORWARD**
BY SANDEEP RAVIDUTT SHARMA

Give your best today and insecurities are no more.

© **THE WAY TO GO IS FORWARD**
BY SANDEEP RAVIDUTT SHARMA

Panic befriends negativity. Light the torch of positivity again and again to thwart darkness.

You got the power within to shine like the sun. Remove accumulated dust of negativity and bring your willpower to the fore. You are here to win.

The helpful hand of God is on its way to touch and soothe the distressed soul. Have faith and change your fate.

© **THE WAY TO GO IS FORWARD**
BY SANDEEP RAVIDUTT SHARMA

Your team cannot win unless you all play together.

© THE WAY TO GO IS FORWARD
BY SANDEEP RAVIDUTT SHARMA

If life gives you a green signal, it's time to keep going and reach your destination.

One side talk can never lead to conflict resolution.

You can achieve anything provided self-belief dominates your mind.

The path to heaven is visible only to those who created heaven on earth.

During the period of distress, you may fear even your own shadow. Watch your steps forward rather than follow your shadow.

© **THE WAY TO GO IS FORWARD**
BY SANDEEP RAVIDUTT SHARMA

Accept challenges or it rejects you.

Those who know their limits have to learn how to expand it and reach the world.

When you don't have any explanation for a certain result or happening, we generally call it a miracle. Such favourable miracles are generally experienced by people whose mind is dominated by positive and pure thoughts and who are kind. Be positive.

Good and bad times come and go in life. This is just a way, the creator tests, your patience.

© **THE WAY TO GO IS FORWARD**
BY SANDEEP RAVIDUTT SHARMA

You are born lucky and will remain so throughout your life.

© **THE WAY TO GO IS FORWARD**
BY SANDEEP RAVIDUTT SHARMA

The golden glow of the sun appears to bless you everyday. Wake up in time and feel blessed.

© **THE WAY TO GO IS FORWARD**
BY SANDEEP RAVIDUTT SHARMA

Divine Sun doesn't wait for any orders to light the world. Don't shy away when your path is full of goodness, all you have to do express your kindness and humanity is delivered.

God comes in various forms but looks great when he appears as a child. The age of innocence is pure and godly.

www.ingramcontent.com/pod-product-compliance
Lightning Source LLC
Chambersburg PA
CBHW070803220526
45466CB00002B/532